OMGee Good!

SOY CURLS™ RECIPES

Plant-Based Meals for the Whole Family

VOLUME 1

JILL MCKEEVER

Copyright © 2017 by Jill McKeever

All rights reserved. No part of this book may be used or reproduced in any manner whatsoever without written permission except in the case of brief quotations embodied in critical articles or reviews.

Butler Foods, LLC is not affiliated with Jill McKeever or this book series, OMGee Good Soy Curls Recipes: Plant-Based Meals for the Whole Family, Volume 1, 2, and 3.

No company or person, named in this book, paid Jill McKeever to mention or promote them or their products.

ISBN-13: 978-1979008211   ISBN-10: 1979008213

Self-published by Jill McKeever, PO BOX 171201, Austin, TX 78717

Printed in the United States of America

Photography by Jill McKeever, unless otherwise indicated.
Korean Bibimbap photo by Lou Anne Lay, Memaw's Veggie Stew photo by Diane Propson , Grilled Lemon Herb Curls Salad photo by Laurie Johnson
Full cover and book interior design by Vincent Saldaña
Printed by CreateSpace, an Amazon Company

Dedication

To Charles, Max, Maggie, and Poncho,
for your unshakeable support
and willingness to eat a jillion Soy Curls™
with a smile and a wagging tail.

Table of Contents

Letter to Reader 8

Soy Curls™ 101 9

MAIN DISHES 19

    Creamy Alfredo 21

    Indian Butter Soy Curls™ Hold the Butter 23

    Korean Bibimbap 25

    OMGee Good! Meatloaf 27

    OMGee Good! Sloppy Jill Sandwiches 29

    Quick Soy Curls™ Tacos 31

    Soy Curls™ Verde Enchiladas 33

    Quick Cabbage Rolls in the Instant Pot® 35

    Hot Pepper Soy Curls™ with Rice Noodles 37

    Kid-Friendly Curry with Coconut Milk 38

    Orange Soy Curls™ 39

    Sam's Taco Crumbles™ Crispy Potato Tacos 40

    Sesame-Peanut Noodles and Soy Curls™ 41

    Teriyaki Soy Curls™ 42

SOUPS & STEWS 43

    Memaw's Veggie Stew 45

    Picky Eater's Noodle Soup 47

    Roasted Butternut Stew 48

    Veggie Pho with Soy Curls™ 49

SEASONED & READY TO ROCK! 51

    Breakfast Sausage Crumbles 53

    Garlic Soy Curls™ 55

    Make Ahead Meatballs 57

    Jill's Classic Barbecue Rub 59

    Righteous Soy Curls™ 60

SALADS 61

    Barbecue Curls, Kale and Quinoa 63

    Grilled Lemon Herb Curls Salad 65

    Ginger Soy Curls™ Salad 66

    Indoor Smoked Curls Salad 67

    Loaded Taco Bowl 68

CONDIMENTS & SPICE BLENDS 69

    Fat-Free Salad Oil Substitute 71

    Sweet and Smoky Barbecue Sauce 73

    Ranch-Style Seasoning 74

Nutrition Information 76

Resources 77

Acknowledgments 81

Index 83

About the Author 85

Fan Raves

"Thanks to you we love the soy curls now."
~ PaintedRavensong

"I made Teriyaki Soy Curls on the stove. My adult son who is not a vegetarian came for dinner, ate it without realizing it was meat free. He loved it and said it was just like his favorite Chinese take out. Home run! Thank you for the recipe."
~ Elainea Singleton

"I just love you! You've changed my life. This plant-based journey is so much easier since I found your channel and .... soy curls." ~ Ginny Mullins

""Bought my first soy curls thanks to you a week ago. AWESOME STUFF! My kids and I made your BBQ soy curl recipe, and it was a huge hit. I'm making them again tonight!"
~ Jennifer Douglas-Craig

"Because of you, we can now enjoy barbecue sandwiches that taste great by just using Soy curls! Thanks for showing us this amazing food!" ~ Lynn F.

"As soon as I found your channel a month ago, I saw you were using soy curls, and I bought the 6-bag order. Love them! Also, love your channel and your down to earth personality!"
~ Vera Deringer

Letter to Reader

Thank you for including *OMGee Good! Soy Curls™ Recipes Volume 1, Plant-Based Meals for the Whole Family* to your cookbook collection. I assume your ownership of this book means you are familiar with Soy CurlsTM. You've tried your first bag, or you're a long time user, either way, you're stoked about owning the first Soy CurlsTM cookbook series in the universe! "WOOT WOOT!"

Aside from writing the first Soy Curls™ cookbook, my chief goal behind writing this book was to equip you with meal ideas that would support you in your effort to attract your favorite people over to the plant-based way of life. In my years living plant-based, I've learned a few things about inspiring friends and family. We don't need a degree in nutrition. We don't need to run marathons. We don't have to show graphic movies. We don't have to be at our perfect weight or look like bodybuilders. All it takes to inspire people is to have a great attitude, let people see your joy for this lifestyle, live by example, and share your favorite OMGee good recipes as often as possible. The people who witness your joy and journey, and are ready to make changes in their own lives, will come to you. In the meantime, you just keep on being you. Keep on cooking, sharing, and having fun.

Again, thank you for your support. I look forward to hearing from you and being included in your healthy journey

Your friend,

Jill McKeever

My first exposure to Soy Curls™ was while taking a vegan Thai cooking class back in 2014. The chef showed us a bowl of pale, dry, funky looking, curly things and said, "This is our protein." Without thinking, the child inside me blurted out, "OH, THOSE ARE WEIRD!" Deep down, I was afraid of being grossed out in front of the other kids in class. However, I played it cool as usual.

We learned how to bring those dry, curly things to life, then added them to a coconut curry recipe. When it came time to taste our cooking, the first soy curl bite sent me into a foodie trance. The texture, the tenderness, the chewiness, and its ability to absorb the flavors around it, blew my mind. The possibilities, oh the places I could go, Dr. Suess! I envisioned our old, favorite omnivore meals transformed and set across our dining table with my family's eyes sparkling with hunger and happiness. It was foodie love at first bite.

These days, it's not unusual for me to keep a 12-pound bag of curls (my little nickname) in the second freezer, along with a stash of Harvest Jerky #19 and Sam's Taco Crumbles™. My picky, teenage daughter loves curls and lo mein noodles simmered in broth and mild spices. I taught her how to cook them in the Instant Pot®, and her inner chef was born. My teenage son would eat his weight in Harvest Jerky #19 and Sam's Taco Crumbles™ if I'd let him. Both teens have evolved to cooking more for themselves and the whole family on a weekly basis because of Soy Curls™. (Thank you, LORD!) My husband, Charles, says Soy Curls™ are the plant-based way to a carnivore's heart. He's particularly fond of my barbecue sandwiches made with homemade barbecue sauce and shredded curls. Anytime we have omnivores over for dinner; he votes for Jill's Famous Barbecue Sandwiches to entice our guests over to the plant side. So far, I haven't met an omnivore who wasn't pleasantly surprised and intrigued to try them again.

As you read and cook your way through this book, I want to encourage you to reach out to me when you have questions and praises to share. I am online Monday through Saturday via multiple social media channels. There is a special Facebook page for the book; you can share this OMGee good book with other Soy Curls™ fans and newbies. There's also a Facebook group for Soy Curls™ fans and newbies to discuss best cooking practices, recipes, where to buy, post food pictures, and share stories of family or friends trying and enjoying curls. Links to Facebook pages and social media channels are below. Anytime you have a soy curl-related praise or shout out, please include the following hashtags in your post to alert me, Butler Foods, and other Soy Curls™ fans: #jillmckeever, #butlerfoods, #soycurls, #omgeegood.

Let's get cooking!

P.S.
Post questions and praises to the following social media channels.
Facebook.com/soycurlsrecipes/
Facebook.com/groups/soycurlsrecipes/
Twitter.com/jillmckeever, #jillmckeever, #butlerfoods, #soycurls, #omgeegood
Youtube.com/user/SimpleDailyRecipes

P.S.S.
If you ever get the urge to go old-school and want to mail a letter to me, go for it. I love mail! I have the cutest photo collection of patrons, grandkids, and furry babies wearing bunny ears.
Send mail to: Jill McKeever, P.O. Box 171201, Austin, TX 78717

Soy Curls™ 101

Soy Curls™ are a delicious alternative to meat and an awesome addition to your favorite recipes. Soy Curls™ are 100% natural, contain the whole soybean, high in protein, a good source of fiber, gluten-free, vegan, non-GMO - no chemical pesticides, grown & made in the USA, zero trans fats, low sodium, and no cholesterol.

How Are Soy Curls™ Made?

The soybeans are soaked in pure spring water (no chlorine or fluorine) and then stirred while cooking which elongates the protein strands. It is similar to what happens when we knead dough in making bread except, of course, Soy Curls™ do not contain gluten. This is what develops the texture and is referred to as texturing. There is nothing added and nothing removed from the soybeans. They are very pure. Then they are dried and packed into bags.

Soy Curls™ contain the natural oils which are high in Omega-3 and Omega-6 and do not contain any preservatives or conditioners. The oils will degrade over time and may develop an off flavor. Soy Curls™ are best kept in the refrigerator or freezer.

Prepping Soy Curls™

The simplest way to prep Soy Curls™ is to measure out the amount of Soy Curls™ you need for a recipe, place in an appropriate size bowl then cover with hot water. Allow Soy Curls™ 8 to 10 minutes to absorb the water then drain off any excess water. You're now ready to rock an old favorite recipe.

Rehydrated Soy Curls™ can be left whole, chopped and shredded. Left whole, seasoned with a variety of spices, they are ready to be baked, grilled or dried (think jerky). Chopped Soy Curls™ are perfect for salads, salad-sandwiches, casseroles, soups, and baked hand-pies. Shredded Soy Curls™ are awesome for baked hand-pies, pulled barbecue sandwiches, casseroles, soups, and salads. To shred Soy Curls™, fill a food processor or drink blender half way up with rehydrated Soy Curls™. Set to the absolute lowest speed setting, turn on processor or blender and allow the s-blade or blades to run for 5 seconds. SHAZAM! Shredded Soy Curls™ come out looking like shredded chicken. I kid you not.

Jill's Sorting Method

Now, you can call me a foodie with too much time on my hands, but I have evolved to sorting Soy Curls™ in order to skip past chopping or getting out the food processor. Sorting doesn't take long and can easily be delegated to a kid. Kids are professional sorters, especially those who own Legos.

Watch my YouTube video to learn how I sort Soy Curls™ into four sizes. http://simpledailyrecipes.com/sorting-soycurls

Get out four bowls, four freezer bags, and a crisper sheet or colander with 1/8" diameter holes. On a clean counter, pour out a bag of Soy Curls™ over the sifter. If you have the 12-pound bulk bag, you can scoop out as much as you like. Shake and pick out all the pieces that measure 1 1/4" or longer and place in bowl number one. Next, shake around and pick out all the 3/4" and 1" pieces and place in bowl number two. All that should be left are the 1/4" to 1/2" pieces in the sifter. Place them in bowl number three. Left behind on the counter should be, what I like call "curl dust." Swipe the curl dust into bowl number four.

Grab another bag or scoop of Soy Curls™ and do it all other again. Keep sorting until you have filled any one of the freezer bags.

Label bag number one, "Grill and Jerky Curls" and fill with Soy Curls™ from bowl number one. Label bag number two, "Soup Curls" and fill with Soy Curls™ from bowl number two. Label bag number three, "Salad Curls" Soy Curls™ from bowl number three. Label bag number four, "Curl Dust" and fill with Soy Curls™ from bowl number four. Store all the bags in the freezer until you're ready to use them.

Storing

Dry Soy Curls™ are best kept refrigerated or frozen. If you're considering purchasing the 12-pound bulk bag from ButlerFoods.com, the heavy-duty storage bag included in the order is great at protecting them against freezer burn. I have taken as long as 12 months to empty a 12-pound bag kept in the freezer and had great tasting Soy Curls™ all the way down to the crumbs.

Rehydrated Soy Curls™ keep well refrigerated 3 to 4 days. They can be refrozen after rehydration as well. This is ideal for those times when you want to marinate extra Soy Curls™ for make-ahead meals or batch cooking.

To thaw frozen seasoned/marinated Soy Curls™, transfer to the refrigerator or defrost in a microwave. Frozen, unseasoned, rehydrated Soy Curls™ quickly thaw when placed in a colander and put under running hot water. Shake and gently squeeze out excess water, and you're ready to get a meal going.

Marinating

When using the marinades from this book, follow these steps:
1. Mix marinade in an appropriate size bowl.
2. Pour marinade over dry Soy Curls™. If marinade does not come up to the side of the top of the Soy Curls™, add just enough water to make it happen. Soy Curls™ do not need to be swimming in liquid; barely covered in liquid works well.

3. Allow at least 10 minutes or the designated time for curls to marinate.
4. Drain off and reserve marinade if you're planning on grilling. Reserved marinades are good for basting in the last few minutes of grilling and baking.

Best Cooking Methods

Pan Frying

Start with either rehydrated or marinated Soy Curls™. Cook Soy Curls™ over medium to medium-high heat with vegetables and spices. There's no need to add oil. To prevent food from scorching in the pan, add 1 to 2 tablespoons of vegetable broth or water while cooking. When the vegetables are cooked tender, the Soy Curls™ are ready, too. Soy Curls™ have already been cooked. We only need to rehydrate and season them to use them in our recipes.

Slow Cooking/Pressure Cooking

Dry Soy Curls™ (whole, chopped, or curl dust) can be added to any slow cooker or pressure cooker recipe. Keep in mind that you will need to add a little extra broth or water to the recipe for the Soy Curls™ to absorb. For instance, if you add one cup of dry curls to a pot of soup add an extra 1/2-cup broth or water.

Marinated Soy Curls™ can be added whole, chopped or shredded to any slow cooker or pressure cooker recipe.

You don't have to worry about overcooking Soy Curls™. Chopped, shredded, or crumbled curls work best for slow cooking for up to 8-hours and pressure cooking up to 15-minutes.

Grilling

Dust off your grill skills and get out your old favorite rubs and barbecue sauce recipes. Grilling is my FAVORITE way to cook Soy Curls™. First, you only need a gas-grill to do the job. Charcoal grills are impractical because they take too long to prepare for the short grilling time needed for curls. Soy Curls™ literally takes 10 minutes of grill time to make a barbecue party rock.

Heat your gas grill to between 250° to 300°F. If you have two or more burners, prep cooking area for indirect grilling. You'll need a nonstick grill pan, preferably perforated, or grill basket. I have fashioned a quick pan from heavy-duty aluminum foil that made for an easy clean up afterward.

Lay marinated Soy Curls™ across grill pan. Set grill pan or basket on the cool side of the grill and set a timer for 5 minutes. Do not walk away. Soy Curls™ scorch quickly on the grill. Flipping them can be a tedious step but worth doing. A pair of long tongs works well for moving and flipping the curls without being grilled yourself. Once flipped, slather on a basting sauce, hot wing sauce, or barbecue sauce. Grill 5 more minutes, or until golden brown. Turn off the grill. Remove from heat.

If you don't want to get out the big grill, an indoor grill works just as well. I own a Cuisinart 5-in-1 Griddler with nonstick grill plates and a thoroughly heated surface. It doubles as a griddle and as a panini grill. It's fun to crank her up to high heat, arrange a layer of marinated Soy Curls™ across the grill plates and press them for 5 to 8 minutes until they're lightly golden and sporting sexy grill marks. Oh, mercy! I'm getting hungry just thinking about them! Are you hungry too? Stay with me; don't jump to the recipes just yet.

Baking

You can use a toaster oven or full-size oven for baked Soy Curls™. Heat oven to 350°F. and bake anywhere from 8 to 15 minutes, until lightly golden and chewy, but not dried out. Use a baking sheet lined with a silicone mat to prevent sticking. If you don't have a silicone mat, allow the curls to cool on the baking sheet for 5 minutes or so. They will easily pop off with the help of a spatula. There's no need to grease the sheet.

Convection Oven and Air Frying

I admit air frying is new to me, even as I write this book. It is a newfangled way of cooking and all the rage among online foodies. I own a Breville Smart Oven Air, which is a big, beautiful convection oven with a unique fan for air frying and roasting. She's awesome, and I love her like she's family. Don't judge me.

So with all that said, I'm currently finding great results air frying Soy Curls™ at 325°F for 8 minutes. This temperature and time produce tender, chewy Soy Curls™--not too dry, not too moist--reminiscent of baked chicken strips. Remember those? Anyhoo, marinate or massage the Soy Curls™ with your favorite marinade or dry rub recipes, or toss them in a bowl of seasoned cornstarch, then spread them across a crisper sheet. Air fry at the temperature and time I've already suggested. Again, air frying is new right now, so there are no hard and fast rules to follow. Play around with temperatures and times until you find a combo that works for the recipes you like most.

Making Jerky

Making jerky with Soy Curls™ is SO MUCH easier and faster than traditional jerky. Once you get the hang of drying jerky, you'll want to keep it on hand for snacking and taking on camping trips.

In a medium bowl, whisk marinade ingredients then stir in Soy Curls™. Mix to assure all the Soy Curls™ are evenly coated. Marinate anywhere from 10 to 30 minutes.

Spread curls across dehydrator trays. Dehydrate at 130°F. for 30 to 50 minutes. Turn trays halfway round at the half time mark. Store in an airtight container or resealable bags in the fridge.

DRYING TIP: Separate curls based on length and thickness when arranging on drying trays. The longer, thicker Soy Curls™ typically need a longer drying time, whereas the 1-inch, thinner curls could be dry in 30 minutes. Also, keep the smallest curls grouped close in the center of the tray to prevent them from drying out too quickly. If you have a lot of small (3/4" pieces), you will want to check on them at the 20-minute mark.

SPECIAL NOTE FROM JILL

For the remainder of this book, you will find me referring to Soy Curls™ as curls, curl crumbles, and curl dust. Also, I am an Instant Pot® master, some call me the "Instant Pot® Queen." I own three and use them all the time. There are recipes in this book that include cooking directions for the Instant Pot®, particularly when slow cooking and pressure cooking are involved.

Main Dishes

Creamy Alfredo

Fan Rave! *"Oh my word, this was awesome. Even had it for lunch the next day." ~Teresakitty1*

Makes 8 servings

2 cups Soy Curls™
1 tablespoon Bragg Liquid Aminos or soy sauce
1-pound linguini
1 large cauliflower, roughly chopped
1 small yellow onion, diced
2 large garlic cloves
2 cups vegetarian no-chicken broth
1 cup raw cashews or white beans
1/2 teaspoon sea salt
1/2 teaspoon ground white pepper
1/4 cup fresh flat-leaf parsley, chopped (garnish)

Place Soy Curls™ in a bowl and cover with hot water. Season water with liquid aminos. Soak curls for 10 minutes. Drain and gently press out excess water. Next, place curls in a food processor, set on the lowest speed. Process with 5 quick pulses to make them resemble shredded meat. Set aside.

In a large pot, bring 5 quarts water to a boil on the stovetop. Cook pasta according to its package directions. Drain. Transfer to casserole dish and toss together with shredded curls. Keep warm.

While the pasta is cooking, place the cauliflower, yellow onion, garlic, broth, cashews or white beans, salt, and pepper in a saucepan over medium heat. Cover with a lid. Simmer 5 minutes, or until cauliflower is fork-tender.

Carefully transfer cooked cauliflower mixture to a blender; blend until creamy smooth. Add up to an additional 1/2 cup broth or unsweetened organic soymilk, to thin sauce. Add salt and pepper to taste. Pour cauliflower sauce over the pasta; mix until well coated. Garnish with Italian parsley.

Serve with a leafy green salad and hot garlic bread. Holler, "Dinner!"

Indian Butter Soy Curls™ Hold the Butter

My husband and teen son devour this meal everytime I cook it. The creamy tomato sauce is loaded with our flavorite Indian spices. Serve it with a big bowl of brown rice to round out the meal.

Makes 6 servings

3 cups Soy Curls™
1 medium yellow onion, diced
4 garlic cloves, minced
1 (14-oz.) can light coconut milk
1 (6-oz.) can tomato paste
2 tablespoons garbanzo bean flour
2 teaspoons garam masala
1 teaspoon mild or hot curry powder
1 teaspoon minced ginger
3/4 teaspoon sea salt
1/2 teaspoon cayenne pepper
1/4 cup fresh cilantro, chopped

Place Soy Curls™ in a bowl and cover with hot water. Soak curls for 10 minutes. Drain and gently press out excess water. Set aside.

On the stovetop: In a large skillet over medium heat, cook onion in 2 tablespoons water; cook until onion is translucent, 5 to 8 minutes. Stir in remaining ingredients, EXCEPT fresh cilantro. Taste for salt and spiciness. Reduce heat to low simmer. Simmer 30 minutes. Transfer to large serving dish; garnish with cilantro.

In an Instant Pot®: Press [SAUTE] button, then [ADJUST] button to set cooking heat to "Less." Cook onion in 2 tablespoons water; cook until onion is translucent, 5 to 8 minutes. Stir in remaining ingredients, EXCEPT fresh cilantro. Taste for salt and spiciness. Press [Keep Warm/Cancel] button to cancel sauté mode. Press [SLOW COOK] button, then [ADJUST] button to set cooking heat to "Less." Use [-] button to set slow cooking time for 30 minutes. Once cooked, transfer curls and sauce to serving dish; garnish with cilantro. Serve over rice.

Korean Bibimbap

"My children are from South Korea and Bibimbap has long been a family favorite. This recipe gave us back a dish with so many happy memories attached to it. We were laughing, telling stories of trips to Korea and the days our children came home into our waiting arms. When dinner was over, our bellies and our hearts were full!" ~LouAnne L.

Makes 4 to 6 servings

3 cups Soy Curls™, 1 1/2" pieces or longer
2 tablespoons Bragg Liquid Aminos or soy sauce
1/4 cup hot Korean chili paste (gochujang)
2 teaspoon Vegan Fish Sauce (recipe below)
1 teaspoon liquid sweetener
(agave, maple, rice syrup)
1 teaspoon rice vinegar

1 large onion, diced
4 cups kale, shredded
2 cups carrots, julienned
2 cups broccoli florets
1 cup shiitake mushrooms
cooked brown rice for serving

Cover curls with hot water; season water with liquid aminos. Soak curls 10 minutes; drain well.

In a small bowl, mix chili paste with 2 tablespoons water, vegan fish sauce, sweetener and vinegar. Set aside.

In a large skillet or wok over medium heat, cook curls until they start to brown, 5 minutes. Pour on chili sauce; cook 5 minutes. Transfer to serving dish; keep warm.

In the same skillet/wok, sauté onion, kale, carrots, broccoli and mushrooms individually. Use a few tablespoons of water or broth with 1 teaspoon liquid aminos to season vegetables. Sauté until veggies reach desired tenderness. Transfer to individual serving bowls. Keep warm. Serve with cooked brown rice.

> Vegan Fish Sauce
> (Makes 1 cup)
> In a saucepan, simmer 3 cups water, with 1/4 cup shiitake mushrooms, 3 tablespoons salt, and 2 tablespoons soy sauce over medium heat until reduced by half. Strain, cool, and store in the fridge for up to three weeks.

OMGee Good! Meatloaf

Trust me when I say this recipe is OMGee good the next day. Right out of the oven, it's a moist loaf. Once it has spent the night in the fridge, it becomes the solid meaty meal you remember and love. It makes awesome meatloaf sandwiches, too. Oh my word!

Makes 6 servings

- 1 1/2 cups Soy Curls™ dust and small crumbles
- 1 1/4 cup water
- 3 tablespoons Bragg Liquid Aminos or soy sauce
- 1/4 teaspoon liquid smoke
- 2 garlic cloves, minced
- 2 celery stalks, finely chopped
- 1 medium yellow onion, finely chopped
- 10-oz. extra-firm tofu, drained
- 1 1/4 cups rolled oats
- 2 tablespoons stone ground mustard
- 2 tablespoons organic ketchup, plus more for topping
- 2 teaspoons dried parsley
- 1/2 teaspoon dried cracked rosemary
- 1/2 teaspoon dried thyme
- 1/2 teaspoon dried rubbed sage
- 1/4 teaspoon ground black pepper

In a large mixing bowl, soak curl dust and crumbles in water, liquid aminos, and liquid smoke for 8 minutes.

In a large skillet over medium heat, cook garlic, celery, and onion for 3 minutes, then add 1/4 cup water to prevent browning, cook another 3 minutes, until onion is translucent. Remove from heat.

Preheat oven to 375°F.

Once curls are rehydrated, crumble tofu over them; stir in oats, mustard, ketchup. Add spices and cooked veggies. With a clean hand, mash, squeeze and stir until well mixed. Spread meatloaf evenly into a silicone 8x4-inch loaf pan.

Bake 25 minutes. Remove from oven; drizzle top with as much ketchup as you like. Return to oven.

Continue baking another 25 minutes. Allow cooling 15 minutes before cutting into it. This loaf is moist after baking. A night in the fridge firms it up perfectly. If you have the time, make it a day ahead. Slice it up and reheat it either in the microwave or toaster oven.

Cold leftover meatloaf is excellent! Hopefully, you will have leftovers to enjoy the next day.

OMGee Good! Sloppy Jill Sandwiches

I cannot wait for you to taste how the spices and heat from Sam's Taco Crumbles™ balance with the organic ketchup and molasses. The liquid smoke, well, I am a full-blooded plant-based Texan. Where there's veganized meaty meals, there's me with a bottle of liquid smoke. I purposely doubled this recipe with the plan to divide and freeze for future meals. I look forward to reading your online praises after you make these OMGee Good! Sloppy Jill Sandwiches.

Makes 10 to 12 servings

1 (9.5-oz.) bag Sam's Taco Crumbles™
4 cups warm water
2 1/2 cups organic ketchup*
3 tablespoons organic molasses
2 teaspoons pecan liquid smoke
whole wheat burger buns

In a large pot over medium heat, mix the crumbles, water, ketchup, molasses, and liquid smoke. Bring to a boil, then reduce heat to medium-low to a gentle simmer. Cover with lid; simmer for 10 to 15 minutes. Fill each bun with about 3/4 cup Sloppy Jill filling. Serve hot.

Divide leftover filling into sandwich portions and store in airtight bags in the freezer. It keeps well for up to three months. Thaw overnight in the fridge or remove from plastic bag, place in a bowl, and reheat in a microwave set to 70% power for 5 minutes, or until hot.

*Organic ketchup usually contains fewer sweeteners. If all you have on hand is sweet ketchup, then cut the amount of molasses in half.

Quick Soy Curls™ Tacos

Makes 8 tacos

2 cups vegetable broth
2 cups Soy Curls™, coarsely crumbled
1 small yellow onion, diced
2 teaspoons chili powder
1 teaspoon ground cumin
1 teaspoon oregano
1/4 teaspoon ground black pepper
1/4 teaspoon sea salt
1 (14.5-oz.) can fire-roasted diced tomatoes with green chiles
8 taco shells or tortillas
1 1/2 cups tomato, chopped
1 1/2 cups lettuce, shredded
1 large avocado, mashed

In a large skillet over medium heat, bring vegetable broth to a simmer. Add crumbled curls and diced onion. Cook 5 minutes or until onion is tender. Stir in chili powder, cumin, oregano, pepper, salt, and roasted diced tomatoes with juice. Simmer 10 minutes.

Bake taco shells according to directions on the package. Fill each taco shell with soy curl filling, and top with tomato, lettuce, and avocado.

Soy Curls™ Verde Enchiladas

Makes 6 servings

2 cups Soy Curls™
1 tablespoon Bragg Liquid Aminos or soy sauce
3 cups potato, cut into small cubes
1 (4-oz.) can diced green chiles
1 cup yellow onion, finely diced
1 cup green bell pepper, finely diced
1 small jalapeño, seeds removed, finely diced
1 cup vegetarian no-chicken broth
1 1/2 teaspoons oregano

1 1/2 teaspoons ground cumin
1/4 teaspoon sea salt
1/4 teaspoon ground black pepper
4 cups fresh spinach, chopped
12 tortillas, flour or corn, warmed to be pliable
2 (14-oz.) cans Hatch Green Chile Enchilada Sauce, mild
1 (2.25-oz) can sliced black olives, drained

Place curls in a bowl and cover with hot water; season with 1 tablespoon liquid aminos. Soak curls 10 minutes. Drain and gently press out excess water. Place curls in a food processor with an S-blade or in a drink blender. On the slowest of slow settings, run the processor for 5 seconds to shred. Transfer to a bowl; set aside.

In a large deep skillet over medium heat, cook potato, green chiles, onion, bell pepper, jalapeño, vegetarian no-chicken broth, shredded curls, oregano, cumin, salt, and pepper for 10 minutes, or until potato is fork tender. Stir in spinach; cook 2 minutes.

Preheat oven to 375°F.

Fill each tortilla with about 3 to 4 tablespoons filling; roll up and lay seam side down in 9-inch by 13-inch casserole dish. Pour Green Chile Enchilada Sauce over enchiladas. Top with black olives. Bake 30 minutes.

Quick Cabbage Rolls in the Instant Pot®

If you ever want to do something different with leftover meatloaf, try using it to fill cabbage rolls. It makes surprisingly good cabbage rolls. If you don't have leftover meatloaf, but want to use your iPot to make cabbage rolls, then mix up the filling from the Old School Cabbage Rolls recipe instead. Follow the pressure cooking directions here, and you'll have a favorite family meal to add to your menu planner.

Serves 4 to 6

1 small head green cabbage, core removed
2 cups leftover OMGee Good! Meatloaf, crumbled (page 27)
2 cups leftover cooked brown rice
1 (24-ounce) jar marinara sauce
1 cup water
1 small carrot, finely shredded
1 1/2 cups thick soy yogurt

Place the cored cabbage on a trivet in the Instant Pot® inner pot; add 1 cup water. Lock on lid; turn steam release handle to "Sealing." Press [MANUAL] button to activate pressure cooking mode; use [- or +] button to adjust cooking time to 1 minute. After cooking time is finished, carefully turn steam release handle to "Venting" for quick pressure release. Once all the steam is released, the lid will unlock automatically, then you can remove the lid. Carefully move cabbage, core side up, to plate to cool enough to handle. Remove trivet and discard cooking liquid.

To separate cabbage leaves, pull leaves away from the center like you're opening a flower blossom. Once you have the very center of the cabbage exposed, where the leaves are too small for rolling, remove the center bunch. It may not be entirely cooked tender. That's okay; chop it up. You will use the chopped cabbage to layer the bottom of the inner pot when it's time to stack the inner pot with cabbage rolls.

With a paring knife, shave off the thick back rib of each cabbage leaf and stack leaves on a plate. Once all the cabbage leaves are prepped. Finely chop all the cabbage ribs and toss with the chopped cabbage.

In the inner pot, cover bottom with 1 cup hot water and a third of the marinara sauce. Layer the bottom with the chopped cabbage.

In a mixing bowl, combine crumbled meatloaf with brown rice. Lay a cabbage leaf, rib side down, fill with 1/4 cup meatloaf mixture. Roll up into leaf, tucking the sides in to secure filling from falling out the sides. Continue filling and rolling until the meatloaf mixture is all used. Any leftover cabbage leaves can be chopped and added to the bottom of the pot.

Stack cabbage rolls in the inner pot, cover with marinara sauce. Lock on lid; turn steam release handle to "Sealing." Press [MANUAL] button to activate pressure cooking mode; use [- or +] button to adjust cooking time to 2 minutes. After cooking time is finished, wait 5 minutes then carefully turn steam release handle to "Venting." Once all the steam is released, the lid will unlock automatically, then you can remove it.

Use a slotted spoon to carefully move cabbage rolls to a serving dish. Ladle sauce around rolls. Serve with soy yogurt.

Hot Pepper Soy Curls™ with Rice Noodles

Makes 2 servings

1 1/2 cups Soy Curls™
2 tablespoons Bragg Liquid Aminos or soy sauce
2 tablespoons Hoisin Sauce
1 tablespoon Asian chili-garlic sauce
1/2 teaspoon liquid sweetener (agave, maple, rice syrup)
3 bundles (8-oz. package) rice noodles
1 large garlic clove, finely chopped
1 red bell pepper, cut into 1-inch pieces
1 small onion, cut into 1-inch pieces
1/2 cup fresh basil leaves, preferably Thai basil

Place Soy Curls™ in a bowl and cover with hot water. Season water with 1 tablespoon liquid aminos. Soak curls for 10 minutes. Drain and gently press out excess water. Set aside.

In a small bowl, whisk 1 tablespoon liquid aminos, hoisin sauce, chili-garlic sauce, and sweetener; set aside.

In a medium saucepan filled with 4 cups water, bring to a boil to cook the rice noodles according to the directions on its package. Drain; set aside.

In a wok over medium heat, cook garlic for 1 minute. Add curls, bell pepper, onion, and 3 tablespoons water. Stir-fry until vegetables begin to soften, 5 to 8 minutes. Add noodles, sauce, and basil; toss until noodles and vegetables are well coated. Cook 2 minutes to heat through.

Get out the chopsticks and bowls and holler, "Dinner time!"

Kid-Friendly Curry with Coconut Milk

"I made Kid-Friendly Curry with Coconut Milk. My first time using soy curls. It's delicious! I can't even describe how fun vegan cooking is now that I have found you, Jill. This dish was an absolute hit, and there is only two of us. We had it last night for dinner, and when I went to have some for lunch today the hubby had eaten the rest already! (And I don't even care because he LIKED it!) Woot Woot!" ~ Mary Ellen Wagenman

Makes 4 servings

- 2 1/2 cups Soy Curls™, 1" pieces
- 1 cup yellow onion, finely diced
- 5 garlic cloves, minced
- 2 teaspoons mild curry powder
- 1 teaspoon garam masala
- 1/2 teaspoon whole cumin seeds
- 1/2 teaspoon ground coriander
- 2 large ripe tomatoes, diced
- 4 cups fresh spinach, roughly chopped
- 1 cup light coconut milk
- 1 cup water
- 2 medium potatoes, peeled, diced small
- 1/4 cup fresh cilantro, chopped
- cooked brown basmati rice for serving

Place Soy Curls™ in a bowl and cover with hot water. Soak curls for 10 minutes. Drain and gently press out excess water. Set aside.

On the stovetop: Heat a large deep skillet, over medium heat. Add onion, garlic, plus 3 tablespoons water; cook for 1 minute. Add curry powder, garam masala, cumin seeds and coriander; mix well, cooking 1 minute. Stir in tomato, coconut milk, water, curls, and potato. Cover pan; simmer over medium-low heat 15 minutes, or until the potatoes are tender. Stir occasionally to prevent sticking. Before serving, stir in fresh cilantro. Serve with brown basmati rice.

In the Instant Pot®: Place all the ingredients into the inner pot, except fresh cilantro; mix well. Lock on lid; turn steam release handle to "Sealing." Press [MANUAL] button to activate pressure cooking mode; use [-] or [+] button to adjust cooking time to 2 minutes. After cooking time is finished, wait 10 minutes then carefully turn steam release handle to "Venting." Once all the steam is released, the lid will unlock automatically, then you can remove the lid. Stir in fresh cilantro and serve with brown basmati rice.

Orange Soy Curls™

"My husband absolutely loved it. He gave it two thumbs up. I really liked the orange zest, very nice." ~ Vanessa Anderson

Makes 6 servings

2 cups brown jasmine rice
2 cups Soy Curls™
1 large carrot, julienned
1 large red bell pepper, julienned
1 1/2 cups orange juice
1/4 cup low-sodium soy sauce
2 tablespoons cornstarch
1 tablespoon minced ginger
1 -3 teaspoons Sambal Oelek sweet chili paste
2 large garlic cloves, crushed
1 tablespoon orange zest
1 large scallion, thinly sliced

Cook jasmine rice according to directions on package. Cover to keep warm; set aside.

Meanwhile, place Soy Curls™ in a bowl; cover with hot water. Soak curls for 10 minutes. Drain and gently press out excess water. Set aside.

In a bowl, whisk orange juice, liquid aminos, cornstarch, ginger, chili paste and crushed garlic. Mix in orange zest. Set aside

In a wok over medium-high heat, cook curls until lightly browned, 5 minutes. Transfer to warm bowl. Stir-fry celery, carrots, and bell pepper in 2 tablespoons of water. Cook until veggies are crisp-tender, 5 minutes. Add back in browned curls. Pour orange mixture over vegetables and toss until sauce thickens and comes to boil about 2 minutes. Top with sliced scallion and serve with rice.

Sam's Taco Crumbles™ Crispy Potato Tacos

Makes 2 to 4 servings

1 cup Sam's Taco Crumbles™
1 small yellow onion, diced
2 garlic cloves, minced
2 medium red potatoes, boiled or steamed and diced
1/2 cups vegetable broth, divided
1 teaspoon chili powder
1/2 teaspoon smoked paprika
4 crunchy taco shells
1 avocado, diced
salsa

In a small bowl, soak crumbles in 1/2 cup warm water until water is absorbed, 8 minutes.

In a large skillet over medium-high heat, cook crumbles and onion, 5 minutes, until onion is translucent. Add garlic, potatoes, broth, chili powder, and paprika. Stir and cook 6 to 8 minutes until broth has evaporated. Remove from heat. Divide filling among taco shells. Serve with diced avocado and salsa.

Sesame-Peanut Noodles and Soy Curls™

Makes 6 servings

3 cups Soy Curls™, 1 1/2" pieces or longer

1 (9.5-oz.) package Soba noodles

1 large carrot, shredded

4 green onions, sliced

2 garlic cloves, whole

1 1/2 tablespoons minced ginger

2 tablespoons rice vinegar

2 tablespoons liquid sweetener (agave, maple, rice syrup)

3/4 cup creamy peanut butter

1/2 cup low-sodium soy sauce

1/3 cup warm water

1 to 2 teaspoons Sambal Oelek sweet chili paste

1 1/2 cups cucumber, peeled, julienned

1/2 cup fresh cilantro, chopped

1/4 cup sesame seeds, toasted or natural

Place curls in a bowl and cover with hot water. Season water with 2 tablespoons. Soak curls for 10 minutes. Drain and gently press out excess water. Set aside.

Cook the noodles according to the directions on its package. Drain, transfer to large mixing bowl. Add shredded carrots and half of the green onions; toss gently. Set aside.

In a small cup food processor, blend smooth the garlic, minced ginger, vinegar, sweetener, peanut butter, soy sauce, water, and chili paste. If it is too thick, add up to 2 to 3 tablespoons water to thin to sauce consistency. Set aside.

In a large skillet over medium heat, cook curls until lightly golden, 5 to 8 minutes. Add 1/4 cup peanut sauce; simmer 2 minutes. Pour over noodles.

Serve remaining green onions, cucumber, cilantro, and sesame seeds in individual serving dishes. Allow diners to add their own toppings.

Teriyaki Soy Curls™

Makes 6 servings

3 cups Soy Curls™, 1" pieces or longer
1 small yellow onion, diced
1/2 cup + 2 tablespoons soy sauce
1/2 cup rice vinegar
1/3 organic sugar or brown rice syrup
1 1/4 cups water
1 tablespoon cornstarch
1/4 cup sesame seeds
6 cups cooked brown rice for serving

Place curls in a bowl and cover with hot water. Season water with 2 tablespoons soy sauce. Soak curls for 10 minutes. Drain and gently press out excess water.

In a large wok over medium-high heat, cook curls until lightly golden, 5 to 8 minutes. Transfer to a warm plate. Cook onion in 1 tablespoon water until tender, 5 minutes.

Whisk soy sauce, rice vinegar, sugar, and water. Add to wok and simmer for 3 minutes. Dissolve cornstarch in 2 tablespoons cold water and whisk into the sauce to thicken. Add browned curls back to pan. Stir in sesame seeds. Remove from heat and serve with cooked brown rice.

Soups & Stews

Memaw's Veggie Stew

Memaw's Veggie Stew was the first classic stew I learned to make into a plant-based meal. When Soy Curls™ came into our lives, I was able to recreate my Memaw's chicken and vegetable stew. Soy Curls™ make it easy to bring back old family favorites.

Makes 6 to 8 servings

- 1 medium yellow onion, diced
- 3 large carrots, diced
- 3 celery stalks, diced
- 1 1/2 teaspoons dried parsley
- 1/2 teaspoon dried oregano
- 1 bay leaf
- 1 (14.5-oz.) can diced tomatoes
- 6 medium red potatoes, cubed
- 2 cups whole kernel corn, fresh, canned, or frozen
- 8 cups vegetarian no-chicken broth
- 2 cups Soy Curls™, 1/2" or smaller pieces
- 1 cup frozen green peas, thawed

On the stovetop: In a soup pot over medium-high heat, cook onion, carrots and celery in a 1/4 cup water for 8 minutes. Add all the remaining ingredients. Bring to a boil; reduce heat to simmer. Cover with lid and cook for 30 minutes, occasionally stirring, until potatoes are fork-tender. Remove bay leaf. Stir in thawed green peas and simmer 5 more minutes.

In the Instant Pot®: Add all the ingredients to the inner pot. Lock on lid; turn steam release handle to "Sealing." Press [MANUAL] button to activate pressure cooking mode; use [- or +] button to set cooking time to 2 minutes. After cooking time is finished, wait 10 minutes then carefully turn steam release handle to "Venting." Once all the steam is released, lid will unlock automatically, then you can remove lid. Remove bay leaf. Stir in thawed green peas; allow time to for peas to heat through.

Serve with fresh baked whole grain bread or crackers. Memaw's Veggie Stew keeps well in the freezer for make-ahead meals.

Jill's notes: When preparing vegetables, take care to dice vegetables the same size to ensure even cooking.

Picky Eater's Noodle Soup

My picky, teenage daughter likes to whip up this soup in the Instant Pot® when it's her night to cook. It's simplicity hits the spot.

Makes 2 servings

4 cups vegetarian no-chicken broth
1 cup Soy Curls™, 1" or small pieces
1/2 teaspoon mild curry powder
1/4 teaspoon dried marjoram
1/4 teaspoon dried basil
2-oz. lo mein noodles, broken into thirds
3 cups packed fresh baby spinach, roughly chopped
1/2 cup unsweetened organic soymilk (optional)

In a medium saucepan over medium-high heat, bring broth, curls, and herbs to a boil for 5 minutes. Stir in noodles and spinach; cover with a lid and remove from heat. Allow noodles to soften in the hot broth for 10 minutes. For a creamy noodle soup, add soymilk before serving. It will help to cool the soup as well.

Roasted Butternut Stew

Makes 6 servings

1 medium onion, quartered
1 large red bell pepper, stem and seeds removed
1 1/2 cups butternut squash, cubed
6 cups vegetable broth
1 (14.5-oz.) can diced tomatoes
2 cups Soy Curls™, 1/2" or smaller pieces
2 cups cooked kidney beans, drained
1 cup whole kernel corn, fresh, canned, or frozen
1 tablespoon Bragg Liquid Aminos or soy sauce
1 1/2 teaspoons chili powder or smoked paprika
1/2 teaspoon ground cumin
1/2 teaspoon garlic powder
1/2 teaspoon ground black pepper
1/2 teaspoon liquid smoke

Preheat oven to 425°F. Roast onion, bell pepper, and butternut squash on a baking sheet lined with a silicone mat for 25 minutes, or until squash is fork tender. Allow cooling. Dice onion and bell pepper; set aside.

On the stovetop: In a soup pot over medium heat, add roasted vegetables, and the remaining ingredients. Bring to a boil; lower heat to simmer for 30 minutes. Stir occasionally.

In the Instant Pot®: Add the roasted vegetables and the remaining ingredients to the inner pot. Press [SAUTE] button to activate sauté mode; use the [ADJUST] button to adjust cooking heat to "Less." Simmer 20 minutes occasionally stirring.

Serve with green salad and cornbread.

Veggie Pho with Soy Curls™

This is my personal FAVORITE quick soup. I can literally eat it every day for a week. The trick is having all the veggies prepped ahead time. I whip up the broth, throw the veggies and noodles, divide the greens, then bring it all together. I'm getting hungry just writing about it.

Makes 2 to 3 servings

2 stick pouches of Savory Choice Pho Veggie Broth Concentrate*
1 cup Soy Curls™, 1" pieces
4 bundles rice vermicelli noodles
4 small white button mushrooms, thinly sliced
1 cup broccoli florets, cut into bite-sized pieces
1/2 cup grated carrot

2 teaspoons minced ginger
4 cups packed fresh baby spinach
2 cups packed Napa cabbage, thinly sliced
1/2 cup fresh cilantro, chopped
2 large green onion, sliced
Sriracha hot chili sauce (optional)
Sambal Oelek fresh chili paste (optional)

In a soup pot over medium-high heat, whisk 5 cups water and Pho Veggie Broth Concentrate. Stir in curls and bring to a boil. Add rice vermicelli noodles, mushrooms, broccoli florets, carrot and ginger; reduce heat to low simmer. Simmer 3 minutes. Remove from heat.

Divide spinach, cabbage, cilantro, and green onion among two large individual soup bowls. Using tongs, divide hot noodles among bowls. Ladle hot broth and cooked veggies over noodles and greens. Wait several minutes for the broth to wilt the greens and cool enough to enjoy. Serve with Sriracha and/or Sambal Oelek for a kick of heat in your bowl.

If you can't find Savory Choice Pho Veggie Broth Concentrate, substitute with 4 cups low-sodium vegetable broth.

Fan Raves

"I just bought the soy curls, and they are awesome. Even m :) FYI: I got the 12-pound bulk box. Happy happy joy joy!"
~ Marjorie Colao-Pullman

"My non-vegan husband absolutely loves Butler Foods Soy Curls, all thanks to your wonderful recipes!" ~ Misty Wickett

"I bought Soy Curls because of your videos, and I have to say these are a game changer. So freaking perfectly textured. I really miss white chicken chili, and these things are gonna fix all that. Thank you so much for turning me on to Soy Curls." ~ calonstanni

"OMG!!! I love soy curls and your "meatloaf" recipe rocks! I've made it several times."
~ sweekcake405

"I ordered an Instant Pot®, and Soy Curls then started learning how to cook the plant-based way. I love how delicious the Creamy Alfredo was and how much my family and friends enjoyed it. Yummy!" ~ Karla Horelica

"Thank you, Jill. Just tried soy curls for the first time. I could kiss your face off right now!"
~ Sharon Cooper

Seasoned & Ready to Rock!

Breakfast Sausage Crumbles

These crumbles work anywhere you want to add an extra kick of spice, such as breakfast tacos, cornbread, soups, over hash browns. Let your imagination run wild.

Makes 1 cup

3/4 cup Soy Curls™, finely crumbled
1/4 cup Breakfast Sausage Spice Blend (recipe below)
3/4 cup hot water
1/2 teaspoon liquid smoke

In a mixing bowl, mix crumbled curls and spice blend. Season hot water with liquid smoke; pour over dry mix. Wait 10 minutes for curls to absorb all the liquid.

Heat a nonstick skillet over medium heat, spread soy curl mixture to a 1/2 inch thick pancake. Cook 5 minutes, or until pancake loosens from pan and can be flipped. Flip and cook another 4 minutes. Use a spatula to break up into crumbles, cook crumbles 2 to 3 minutes. Remove from heat.

Breakfast Sausage Spice Blend
Makes 1/4 cup

2 tablespoons flaxseeds
1 teaspoon light brown sugar
1/2 teaspoon sea salt
1/4 teaspoon dried thyme leaves
1/4 teaspoon dried crushed rosemary leaves
1/4 teaspoon fennel seeds
1/4 teaspoon freshly ground black pepper
1/8 teaspoon cayenne pepper
1/8 teaspoon ground nutmeg
1/8 teaspoon dried rubbed sage

Use a spice/coffee grinder to blend all the ingredients into a powder. Use right away for the Breakfast Sausage Crumbles recipe or store in a jar with a lid in the fridge until needed. Refrigeration is necessary to keep the ground flaxseeds from turning rancid.

Garlic Soy Curls™

Makes 2 cups

2 large garlic cloves
1 tablespoon Bragg Liquid Aminos or soy sauce
1/4 teaspoon pecan liquid smoke
2 tablespoons nutritional yeast flakes
1/8 teaspoon ground black pepper
2 cups Soy Curls™, 1 1/2" or longer pieces

In a blender, blend garlic, liquid aminos, liquid smoke with 1 cup warm water. Transfer to medium bowl, add curls and an additional 1/2 cup warm water. Soak curls for 10 minutes. Drain and gently squeeze out excess water. Toss curls with nutritional yeast flakes.

Use the following chart to set heat and cooking time according to the appliance of your choice. Spread marinated curls evenly across a baking sheet. If using an air fryer, you may have to work in batches. Cooked curls store well in the fridge for several days.

Cooking Chart			
Appliance	Temperature	Cook Time	Cook Tray
Air Fryer	325°F	5 minutes	fry basket or crisper tray
Convection Oven	325°F	5 minutes	baking sheet
Oven	325°F	10 minutes	baking sheet
Griddle or Grill Pan	Medium-High	4 minutes each side	n/a

Make Ahead Meatballs

My teen son gobbles these up! They are best eaten the next day and swimming in a good spaghetti sauce.

Makes 24 meatballs

3 garlic cloves, minced
2 celery stalks, finely chopped
1 medium onion, finely chopped
1 1/2 cups Soy Curls™, finely crumbled
3 tablespoons Bragg Liquid Aminos
1/4 teaspoon liquid smoke
10-oz. extra-firm tofu, drained

1 1/4 cups rolled oats
2 teaspoons dried parsley
1/2 teaspoon fennel seeds
1/2 teaspoon dried rosemary
1/2 teaspoon dried thyme
1/2 teaspoon dried rubbed sage
1/8 teaspoon ground black pepper

In a skillet over medium heat, cook garlic, celery, and onion for 4 minutes, add 2 tablespoons water to prevent browning, cook another 3 minutes, until onion is translucent. Remove from heat.

In a mixing bowl, soak curls in 1 1/4 cup water, liquid aminos, and liquid smoke for 8 minutes. Crumble tofu over curls; add oats. With a clean hand, mash and mix until well combined.

Use a spice grinder to blend the spices into a fine powder. Sprinkle over soy curl mixture; add the cooked garlic, celery, and onion. Using your hand, mix until the spices are evenly distributed. Cover and chill for at least 1 hour. The spices grow stronger the longer the mixture is refrigerated.

Preheat oven to 350°F. Line baking sheet with parchment paper or a silicone mat. Use a 1-inch dough scoop to control portion size. Use the palm of your hand to press out the air and pack the mixture into the scoop. This step will make a firmer patty and only leave one hand messy. Drop meatballs onto a baking sheet one inch apart.

Bake 25 minutes. Meatballs will be soft in the center. The chewy, meaty texture, we know, and love comes when the meatballs are allowed to cool completely. Transfer the meatballs to a container and store in the fridge overnight. When you're ready to add them to spaghetti sauce, add cold meatballs to hot sauce. Simmer until hot, about 5 minutes. If you need to stir the sauce, stir gently so as not to break the meatballs

Jill's Classic Barbecue Rub

Makes 1 cup

1/4 cup sea salt
1/4 cup dark brown sugar
1/4 cup smoked paprika
3 tablespoons fresh ground black pepper
1 tablespoon garlic granules
1 tablespoon dried onion flakes
1/2 teaspoon cayenne pepper
1/4 teaspoon ground celery seeds

Mix all the ingredients together. Store in an airtight container away from light and heat. Rub will keep for several months.

Righteous Soy Curls™

When you plan to make Baked Smoky BBQ Curls and Sweet and Smoky Barbecue Sauce, put them together for a most blessed experience.

Makes 8 servings

1 (8-oz.) bag Soy Curls™
3 tablespoons Bragg Liquid Aminos or soy sauce
1 teaspoon liquid smoke
1/4 cup + 1 teaspoon Jill's Classic Barbecue Rub (page 59)
2 cups Sweet and Smoky Barbecue Sauce (page 73)

Place curls in a bowl and cover with hot water. Season water with liquid aminos and liquid smoke. Soak curls 10 minutes. Drain and gently squeeze out excess water. Massage 1/4 cup barbecue rub into curls.

Use the following chart to set heat and cooking time according to the appliance of your choice. Spread marinated curls evenly across a baking sheet. If using an air fryer, you may have to work in batches. After the cooking time, brush the curls with the barbecue sauce. Return coated curls to cook 3 to 5 more minutes. Transfer curls to a platter. Sprinkle with 1 teaspoon rub and serve the remaining sauce on the side.

Cooking Chart			
Appliance	Temperature	Cook Time	Cook Tray
Air Fryer	325°F	5 minutes	fry basket or crisper tray
Convection Oven	325°F	5 minutes	baking sheet
Oven	325°F	10 minutes	baking sheet
Griddle or Grill Pan	Medium-High	4 minutes each side	n/a

Salads

Barbecue Curls, Kale and Quinoa

"Easy to make and a great combo of ingredients. This is great served as a sandwich with pickles and corn on the cob on the side." ~Joy J.

Makes 2 servings

3/4 cup Soy Curls™, 1/4 to 1/2" pieces
1 tablespoon Bragg Liquid Aminos or soy sauce
1/2 cup sweet yellow onion, finely diced
2 cups kale, stems removed, chopped
3/4 cup cooked quinoa or brown rice
1/4 cup your favorite barbecue sauce

Place curls in a bowl and cover with hot water. Season water with liquid aminos. Soak 10 minutes. Drain and gently press out excess water. Set aside.

In a skillet over medium heat, cook onion for 2 minutes. Add 3 tablespoons water and kale. Cover and cook until kale starts to wilt, about 5 minutes. Stir in quinoa, soy curls, and barbecue sauce. Cook until heated through. Serve with additional barbecue sauce.

Grilled Lemon Herb Curls Salad

Makes 4 servings

2 1/2 cups Soy Curls™, 1" pieces
2 tablespoons Bragg Liquid Aminos or soy sauce
2 tablespoons Fat-Free Salad Oil Substitute (page 71)
1/4 cup fresh-squeezed lemon juice
2 tablespoons water
2 tablespoons red wine vinegar
2 tablespoons fresh parsley, chopped
2 teaspoons dried basil
2 teaspoons garlic, minced
1 teaspoon dried Greek oregano
1 teaspoon sea salt
1/4 teaspoon ground black pepper
4 cups Romaine lettuce, torn into bite-sized pieces
1 1/2 -2 cups cucumber, diced
1 cup fresh tomato, diced
1/3 cup garlic-stuffed olives, pitted and sliced
1/4 cup red onion, sliced
1 avocado, cubed
Lemon wedges, to serve

Place curls in a bowl and cover with hot water. Season water with liquid aminos. Soak curls 10 minutes. Drain and press out excess water. Set aside.

Whisk fat-free salad oil substitute, lemon juice, water, vinegar, parsley, basil, garlic, oregano, salt and pepper in a small bowl. Pour half of the dressing over drained curls. Marinate for 15 minutes.

Heat a grill pan or panini grill on medium-high heat. Grill curls on both sides until browned with sexy grill lines, 4 minutes on each side.

In a large salad bowl, toss lettuce, cucumber, tomato, olives, onion, and avocado. Top with grilled marinated curls. Drizzle salad with the remaining dressing. Serve with lemon wedges to squeeze over salad.

Ginger Soy Curls™ Salad

Makes 6 servings

3 cups Soy Curls™, 1/2" to 1" pieces
2 tablespoons Bragg Liquid Aminos or soy sauce
1 package (10.5-oz.) rice vermicelli
4 cups shredded lettuce
1/2 cup shredded carrot
1/4 cup sliced green onions with tops
Ginger Dressing (recipe below)
1 tablespoon toasted sesame seeds

Place curls in a bowl and cover with hot water. Season water with liquid aminos. Soak curls 10 minutes. Drain and gently press out excess water. Set aside.

Boil 4 quarts of water to cook rice vermicelli bundles according to package directions. Drain vermicelli well; transfer half the noodles to large mixing bowl. Toss in curls, lettuce, carrot, and green onion. Pour on ginger dressing and toss until well coated. Place remaining noodles in a serving dish(es), spoon salad over noodles. Sprinkle with sesame seeds.

Ginger Dressing

1/3 cup Fat-Free Salad Oil Substitute (page 71)
1/4 cup white wine vinegar
1 tablespoon maple syrup
1 tablespoon Bragg Liquid Aminos or soy sauce
1 teaspoon minced ginger
1/2 teaspoon ground black pepper

Shake all the dressing ingredients in a tightly covered container. Set aside.

Indoor Smoked Curls Salad

Makes 6 servings

2 1/2 cups Soy Curls™
1/2 cup yellow onion, halved
1 whole garlic clove
1 tablespoon lemon juice
1/2 teaspoon sea salt
1 garlic clove, minced
4 tablespoons Fat-Free Salad Oil Substitute (page 71)
1 teaspoon Tabasco or other hot sauce (optional)
1/2 teaspoon liquid smoke
1 small head Romaine lettuce, torn into pieces
2 medium tomatoes, cut into wedges
2 green onions, sliced
Easy Ranch Dressing (page 74)

In a blender, blend onion, garlic, lemon juice, and salt with 2 cups water. Pour marinade over curls. Soak curls 10 minutes. Drain well.

In the meantime, make smoke baste in a small pan over medium heat, cook garlic until fragrant but not brown, 2 minutes. Remove from heat; stir in fat-free salad oil substitute, hot sauce, and liquid smoke.

Leftovers keep well in the fridge for a week.

Heat a nonstick griddle pan over medium-high heat, brown curls 5 minutes, flip, baste with smoke baste, continue to brown curls 5 minutes. Arrange lettuce and tomatoes on 6 individual plates. Divide grilled curls and top each plate with green onions. Serve with Easy Ranch Dressing.

Loaded Taco Bowl

"This is very good! We were all surprised we liked the yogurt in it. We all agree we would like to try the soy curl mixture on nachos, tacos, rice or in enchiladas." ~ Lou Anne L.

Makes 2 servings

2 large green onions, sliced (white and green parts)
1 garlic clove, minced
1/2 red bell pepper, diced
1 cup Soy Curls™, coarse crumbles
1 cup vegetarian no-chicken broth
1/2 cup whole corn kernels, frozen
1 tablespoon chili powder or paprika
2 teaspoons ground cumin
1/2 teaspoon sea salt
1/2 teaspoon ground black pepper
1 cup cooked quinoa
1/2 cup halved grape tomatoes
1/4 cup fresh cilantro
1/4 cup plain non-dairy yogurt
1/2 jalapeno, sliced
lime wedges (optional)

In a skillet over medium-high heat, cook white parts of green onion, garlic, and bell pepper in 2 tablespoons water for 5 minutes, or until tender. Stir in curls, broth, corn, chili powder, cumin, salt, and pepper. Continue cooking 10 minutes until curls absorb the broth and browning begins. Remove from heat.

Divide quinoa, curls mixture, and remaining ingredients among two bowls. Serve with lime wedges.

Condiments & Spice Blends

Fat-Free Salad Oil Substitute

Fat-free salad oil? NO WAY! Yes way. Pull out all your old favorite oil-based salad dressings recipes. You may enjoy them again. Substitute processed oils one-for-one with this fat-free salad oil substitute.

Makes 1 cup

1 cup low-sodium vegetable broth or water
1 teaspoon cornstarch or arrowroot powder

In a small saucepan over medium-high heat, whisk vegetable broth with cornstarch. Bring to a boil; reduce heat and simmer until the broth goes from cloudy to clear. Takes 5 minutes. Carefully pour hot broth into a heat resistant container, such as a canning jar. Cover with lid. Refrigerate. Once cooled, it has the mouthfeel of salad oil. I kid you not.

Jill's notes: Fat-Free Salad Oil Substitute only works to substitute processed oils in salad dressing recipes and to help herbs and spices cling to Soy Curls™. It is not a substitute for cooking oils used for frying or baking.

Sweet and Smoky Barbecue Sauce

Here's a fantastic barbecue sauce I use to wow carnivores. It's one of my favorites on Soy Curls™, tofu, and tempeh.

Makes 2 1/2 cups

3 tablespoons packed dark brown sugar

1/4 cup apple cider vinegar

2 tablespoons organic molasses

2 tablespoons maple syrup

2 tablespoons Vegan Worcestershire Sauce

1 tablespoon yellow mustard

1/2 tablespoon hickory liquid smoke

1/2 tablespoon smoked hot paprika

1 teaspoon ground black pepper

1 teaspoon garlic granules

1/2 teaspoon ground allspice

1/8 teaspoon ground cloves

2 cups organic ketchup

Combine all the ingredients, except for the ketchup, in a medium saucepan and bring to a simmer over medium heat. Cook, uncovered until all the ingredients are dissolved, constantly stirring, about 5 minutes. Stir in ketchup and bring to a boil, stirring to prevent ketchup from spattering. Reduce the heat slightly to gently simmer the sauce, uncovered, until dark, thick, and richly flavored, about 30 minutes. Stir often. Use right away or transfer to jars, cover, cool to room temperature, and refrigerate. The sauce will keep for several months.

Ranch-Style Seasoning

Yes! You can enjoy Ranch dressing and dip again! This spice blend is great sprinkled over baked potatoes and steamed veggies.

Makes about 1/3 cup

2 tablespoons dried parsley
1 1/2 teaspoons dried dill weed
2 teaspoons garlic granules
2 teaspoons onion granules
2 teaspoons dried onion flakes
1 teaspoon ground black pepper
1 teaspoon dried chives
1/2 teaspoon sea salt (optional)

> **Easy Ranch Dressing**
> 1/2 cup raw cashews
> 1/2 cup water
> 1 tablespoon Ranch-Style Seasoning
>
> Use a small blender to cream cashews, water and seasoning. Chill at least 30 minutes before serving.

Pulse the mixture in a food processor for a more even consistency. Store in an airtight container in a cool, dark place. Keeps well for several months.

Use 1 tablespoon of Ranch-Style Seasoning to every 2/3 cup tofu mayo or soy yogurt. Feel free to add more to suit your liking. Keep in mind spices take time to meld and have the potential to become overpowering. Chill dressing at least 30 minutes before serving.

"Bought soy curls because of you, and now I'm addicted." ~ Dan

"New YouTube subscriber here! I love your upbeat personality, and that your kids love it too! I just ordered Soy Curls because of all your videos, can't wait to try it."
~ hintofmintmeia

"I want to hug your neck just for the soy curls. I am loving making these now that I am cooking for meat eaters more than I used to."
~ Sarah Pauline

"I started a local plant-based group and introduced them to soy curls...they loved them (as do I). Thanks for the great recipes!" ~ Valerie Scrafford

"You got me hooked on Soy Curls, Love them!" ~ Jean Sisk

Nutrition Information

Dry Soy Curls™

Serving Size approximately 3/4 cup, 30g

Servings Per Container approximately 8

Amount Per Serving

Calories 100, Calories from Fat 40

Total Fat 4. 5g

Saturated Fat less than 0. 5g

Cholesterol 0mg

Sodium 5mg

Total Carbohydrate 5g

Dietary Fiber 3g

Sugars 1g

Protein 10g

Sam's Taco Crumbles™

Serving Size approximately 1/2 cup, 50g

Servings Per Container approximately 13

Amount Per Serving

Calories 60, Calories from Fat 25

Total Fat 2. 5g

Saturated Fat less than 1g

Trans Fat 0g

Cholesterol 0mg

Sodium 290mg

Total Carbohydrate 4g

Dietary Fiber 2g

Sugars 1. 5g

Protein 6g

Resources

Shopping for ingredients online is easier than it's ever been. I have two websites I use most, ButlerFoods.com and Amazon.com. I have listed Butler Foods and the Amazon affiliate links to my personal favorite ingredients and appliances. None of the companies I have listed endorse me; that's why I am sharing affiliate links. All affiliate proceeds go to create plant-based cookbooks, videos, and downloadable information used to trumpet the joy and benefits of living a plant-based lifestyle.

Soy Curls™

Butler Foods is an independent, family-owned business and the creators of Soy Curls™. Their site is the best source for stocking up on Soy Curls™, Taco Crumbles™, and other goodies. Soy Curls™ are sold in 8-oz. bags and in a 12-pound bulk box. After my family unanimously voted Soy Curls™ into our weekly meal routine, I went directly to the source to save money.

ButlerFoods.com

Bragg Liquid Aminos

Bragg Liquid Aminos is not fermented, is Gluten-Free, and is made from non-GMO soybeans and purified water. For me, it lends a saltier and smokier flavor than tamari and soy sauce. It contains 320mg of sodium per teaspoon serving. If less sodium is desired, use the 6oz. Bragg Liquid Aminos spray bottle and dilute it (2/3 Bragg Liquid Aminos to 1/3 distilled water) before using or spraying on food. I reach for it to season the water for soaking Soy Curls™.

http://simpledailyrecipes.com/liquid-aminos

Nutritional Yeast Flakes

Nutritional yeast is a deactivated yeast, often a strain of Saccharomyces cerevisiae, which is sold commercially as a food product. It is sold in the form of flakes or as a yellow powder and can be found in the bulk aisle of most natural food stores. It has a strong flavor that is described as nutty, cheesy, or creamy, which makes it popular as an ingredient in cheese substitutes. It is often used by vegans in place of cheese, for example in mashed and fried potatoes, atop of "scrambled" tofu, in a cheese sauce or queso, or as a topping for popcorn.

http://simpledailyrecipes.com/nutritional-yeast-flakes

Tamari

Reduced-sodium tamari is another gluten-free soy sauce I personally like to use it for sauces and dressings. To me, it has a milder flavor than soy sauce. It's widely available in grocery stores, but in case you can't find it, here's the link.

http://simpledailyrecipes.com/tamari

Colgin Liquid Smoke

Colgin is the best maker of natural liquid smoke, hands down. Colgin Natural Liquid Smoke can easily be found in most grocery stores in the condiment section, usually near the BBQ sauces and ketchup. Honestly, I blow through the small 4-oz. bottles sold in the stores and often times the store is out of my favorite flavor of smoke. So, as an attempt to reduce plastic use and ensure I have want I like, I buy apple and pecan liquid smoke by the gallon directly from Colgin. What can I say? We're fans.

Colgin.com

Black Salt

Kala Namak is a volcanic rock salt with a characteristic sulfurous aroma. The taste would remind you of an over-salted hard-boiled egg. It is often used in egg-free dishes to give them flavor reminiscent of eggs. It is commonly found, finely ground by the bag, in Indian grocery stores for a very low price. When ordering online, make sure the description reads "Kala namak." There are other black salts on the market that are in no way similar in flavor.

http://simpledailyrecipes.com/kalanamak

New Mexico Chili Powder

New Mexico Chili Powder is full of chili flavor without all the heat. Check the bulk spice aisle of your local foodie mart before jumping online; you'll save a little money that way. I'm not partial to any particular brand--only the flavor. I go through quite a bit of it and tend to stock up when I come across it.

http://simpledailyrecipes.com/nmchilipowder

Savory Choice Pho Veggie Broth Concentrate

Savory Choice Pho Veggie Broth Concentrate is a liquid broth concentrate made with no MSG, no HVP, no I+G, no preservatives, no trans–fats, and gluten-free and is packed in single-serve foil stick pouches. Each stick pouch of liquid broth concentrate is reconstituted with 2 cups (16 ounces) hot water. Each box contains 4 stick pouches that will make a total of 64 ounces of vegetable pho broth. It's absolutely delicious, and I keep it on hand at all times. The best deal I have found is to stock up from Amazon.

http://simpledailyrecipes.com/savorychoicepho

Vegetarian No-Chicken Broth

Imagine Vegetarian No-Chicken Broth is one, out of two, of the best tasting low-fat, gluten-free, organic, non-GMO broths on the market. When it's on sale, I stock up.

http://simpledailyrecipes.com/imagine-vcb

Better Than Bouillon No-Chicken Base is my family's all time favorite no chicken broth. It has all the flavors we remember and enjoy. Some may find it on the salty side. The directions suggest 1 teaspoon base to 1 cup water. I prefer 1/2 to 3/4 teaspoon base to 1 cup water. It really comes down to what you prefer. Each 8-oz. jar makes 38 cups (9.5 quarts) of broth. I keep several jars on hand at all times.

http://simpledailyrecipes.com/btb-vcb

Air Fryer, Convention Oven, and Toaster Oven

Breville Smart Oven Air is one of the most used appliances in our home. With 13 functions, Toast, Bagel, Broil, Bake, Roast, Warm, Pizza, Proof, Air fry, Reheat, Cookies, Slow Cook, and Dehydrate, she's the reason I rarely turn on my old oven. She has the capacity to bake around a 9-inch by 13-inch casserole dish easily. She has a 2-speed fan (Regular & Super) for more cooking control. The super fan moves a greater volume of air to ensure fast and even roasting, air frying and dehydrating. She's awesome; I love her.

http://simpledailyrecipes.com/breville-air

Instant Pot®

Instant Pot® is my other appliance love. I have evolved to owning three just so I can rock out more than one dinner at the same time it takes to cook one. An Instant Pot® is an electric cooker with the ability to sauté, pressure cook, slow cook, make yogurt, and keep food warm. It is so easy to use, too. I have my teens and hubby using it to pump out meals when I'm busy writing recipes.

http://simpledailyrecipes.com/ipot

NutriBullet

NutriBullet Pro, my favorite handy power blender. Its strength to quickly blend nuts and seeds into creamy sauces makes me want to sing a chorus of "Amazing Grace" every time I use it. In those cooking moments when all I need is a half cup of nut-based cream, I reach for this gal. Oh, and salad dressings, she's perfect for blending dressings. She's super handy for making large smoothies for one as well. The whole family uses her on a daily basis.

http://simpledailyrecipes.com/nutribullet

Acknowledgments

I would first like to thank the Simple Daily Recipes community for encouraging me to write OMGee Good! Soy Curls™ Recipes. Without their unwavering support, this book would not exist. I would not have finished it on schedule without my team of recipe testers, who volunteered their time and expertise to fine tuning many of the recipes. Thank you, Lou Anne Lay, Patti Broussard, Diane Propson, Cammie Bruce, Janet Collins, Desiree Pulley, Joy Jerauld, Laurie Johnson, Sheila Meyer, Chris Hansen, Tess Roth, and Vanessa Anderson, for your honest feedback and ninja culinary skills. I want to thank Lou Anne Lay, Sheila Mayer, and Tess Roth for permission to use their photography in this book. A big hug goes to Amy Johnson for helping edit this book. Big bear hugs of gratitude go to Gloria Bankler, Diane Propson, Tess Roth, Lou Anne Lay, and Amy Johnson for helping proofread the final draft at a moments notice. I am thankful to Vincent Saldana for his creative eye and mad coding skills, which transformed my recipes into paperback and e-books.

When Dan Butler of Butler Foods, Inc. found out I needed to send a meticulous order of Soy Curls™ to the recipe testers, he called me straight away. Dan and his team are AWESOME! They donated the Soy Curls™ we needed to the test recipes. Thank you, thank you, Dan and the Butler Foods team!

I am grateful to Annette Fowler and the members of the "Jill McKeever, Plant-Based Lifestyle Support" Facebook group for continuing to welcome new members, answer their questions and express support and encouragement to all those in need of it. Thank you for keeping the fellow-SHIP afloat (pun intended) while the captain was in the galley.

I want to thank my YouTube subscribers for not giving up on me while I focused more time on writing and less time on producing videos. Thank you for the messages and emails letting me know my absence was noticed, for sharing your excitement for the book, and for lovingly telling me to "Hurry up and get back to the live broadcasts and cooking videos."

I am deeply grateful to my family for their willingness to eat a jillion Soy Curls™. I am thankful for my husband, Charles, for shuttling the teens to all their activities so I could stay home and write in an uninterrupted flow. I am super proud of Max and Maggie for mastering the Instant Pot® and making sure the family had a balanced meal night after night. The freedom to test recipes without the concern of organizing dinner too was a huge blessing. I will admit they have spoiled me. I might as well start the next cookbook, so as not to disrupt their cooking routine.

Finally, publishing cookbooks, producing videos, and maintaining the Simple Daily Recipes website, are made possible with the financial support from the following patrons.

James Campbell	Travis Posey	Ruth Pistell	Angela Webb
Pamela Cowperthwaite	Tawni Casteel	Penny McGuire	Colleen VandenBerg
Mary Hare	Sara Shannon	Kelly Lorang	Joyce Anderson
Debbie Sanders	Ann Lee	Gina Paesani-Smith	Sara Hencke
Shontae Usman	Sharie Marshall	Tracy Palmore	Stacy Read
Orren Gaspard	Kimberly Ylitalo	Donayne Sallee	Janice Counts
Brenda Rawlings	Melissa Paulette	Diana Evers	Rosemary Armstrong
Chandra Wooten	Jennifer Fan	Dee Bolemon	Skippy Smith
Karen Franks	Maria Gastaldi	Rick Califf	Maureen Johnson
Tammy Robertson	Jennifer Watkins	Kay A Gerry	Danielle Teakell
Dar Steinis	Jason Buberel	Susan Vargo	Claire Badcock
Jill Deden	Carissa Lounsbury	Candyce Guerra	Melissa Schiavone
Geoff Nelson	Susan Duke	M Kay Hill	Donna
Louise Placek	Brenda Watzin	Ginny Mullins	Gwen Dixon

Thank you from the bottom of my heart.

Index

A

Air Frying 17

B

Barbecue Curls, Kale and Quinoa 63
Barbecue Sauce 60, 63, 73
beans 21, 48
bell peppers 33, 37, 39, 48, 68
Best Cooking Methods 15
Breakfast Sausage Crumbles 53
broccoli 25, 49
brown Jasmine rice 39
brown rice 23, 25, 35, 38, 42, 63

C

cabbage 35, 36, 49
carrot 25, 35, 39, 41, 45, 49, 66
cashews 21, 74
cauliflower 21
coconut milk 23, 38
Condiments 69
Convection Oven 17,
corn 45, 48, 68
Creamy Alfredo 21
cucumber 41, 65

E

Easy Ranch Dressing 67, 74
enchiladas 33, 68

F

Fat-Free Salad Oil Substitute 65, 66, 67, 71

G

Garlic Soy Curls 55
Ginger Soy Curls Salad 66
green chiles 31, 33
green onions 41, 49, 66, 67, 68
Grilled Lemon Herb Curls Salad 65
Grilling 15

H

Hot Pepper Soy Curls 37

I

Indian Butter Soy Curls Hold the Butter 23
Indoor Smoked Curls Salad 67
Instant Pot 23, 35, 38, 45, 47, 48

J

Jill's Classic Barbecue Rub 59, 60

K

kale 25, 63
Kid-Friendly Curry with Coconut Milk 38
kidney beans 48
Korean Bibimbap 25

L

lettuce 31, 65, 66, 67
Loaded Taco Bowl 68
lo mein noodles 47

M

Make Ahead Meatballs 57
Marinating 14
Memaw's Veggie Stew 45
mushrooms 25, 49

N

non-dairy yogurt 28, 68, 74, 80
noodles 37, 41, 47, 49, 66
nutritional yeast flakes 55

O

olives 33, 65
OMGee Good! Meatloaf 27, 35
OMGee Good! Sloppy Jill Sandwiches 29
orange juice 39
Orange Soy Curls 39

P

Pan frying 15
pasta 21
peanut butter 41
Picky Eater's Noodle Soup 47
potato 33, 38, 40, 45, 74
Prepping Soy Curls™ 12
Pressure Cooking 15, 35, 38, 45

Q

Quick Cabbage Rolls in the Instant Pot 35
Quick Soy Curls Tacos 31

R

Ranch-Style Seasoning 74
rice noodles 37
Righteous Soy Curls 60
Roasted Butternut Stew 48
rolled oats 27, 57

S

Salad 61, 63, 65, 66, 67, 68
Sam's Taco Crumbles Crispy Potato Tacos 40
Sandwiches 29
sausage 53
Sesame-Peanut Noodles and Soy Curls 41
sesame seeds 41, 42, 66
Slow Cooking 15, 18, 23
Soba noodles 41
Soup 43, 45, 47, 48, 49
soymilk 21, 47
Soy Curls Verde Enchiladas 33
spice blend 53, 69, 74
spinach 33, 38, 47, 49
Stew 43, 45, 48
Storing 14
Sweet and Smoky Barbecue Sauce 60, 73

T

taco shells 31, 40
Teriyaki Soy Curls 42
tomato 23, 31, 38, 45, 48, 65, 67, 68
tortillas 31, 33

V

Vegan Fish Sauce 25
Vegan Worcestershire Sauce 73
vegetarian no-chicken broth 21, 33, 45, 47, 68, 79
Veggie Pho with Soy Curls 49

About the Author

Jill McKeever is a cooking instructor, author and trained personal coach with a Certificate in Plant-Based Nutrition from the T. Colin Campbell Foundation. In 2011, she watched the film, Forks Over Knives and decided she did not want to grow old with poor health and live on prescription medications. She adopted a whole food, plant-based diet, dropped 30 pounds, and regained the energy to take care of her family and online career. With her new, healthy lifestyle, Jill transformed right in front of her online followers. Today, Jill inspires and guides thousands of people seeking to transition to a plant-based way of life.

You can find Jill on her YouTube channel, Jill McKeever, Simple Daily Recipes. She produces live broadcasts and videos every week to encourage and guide viewers with advice and tips on their plant-based journeys. She offers personal coaching sessions to those needing support and guidance for transitioning to a plant-based diet, as well as, assist with creating and sustaining healthy habits that lead to accomplishing lifestyle goals.

On a more personal note, Jill has been happily married over 20 years to her supportive husband, Charles. They have two awesome teenagers and the sweetest Shih Tzu dog ever, Poncho. The whole family transitioned to live plant-based in 2011, well, except the dog. (They don't judge.) All Texas born and raised, they reside in Austin, Texas.

Follow Jill McKeever

Live Shows & Cooking Videos: Youtube.com/user/SimpleDailyRecipes
Website: SimpleDailyRecipes.com
Facebook: Facebook.com/SimpleDailyRecipes
Instagram: Instagram.com/jillmckeever

Facebook OMGee Good! Soy Curls™ Cookbook Fans: Facebook.com/soycurlsrecipes/
Facebook Soy Curls™ Fans: Facebook.com/groups/soycurlsrecipes/

Check out Jill's downloadable print-friendly cookbooks here: SimpleDailyRecipes.com/bookshop

Also by Jill McKeever

OMGee Good! Instant Pot® Meals, Plant-Based & Oil-Free

Jill's Plant-Based Thanksgiving Recipes 2016

Jill's Marinades for Soy Curls & Soy Curls Jerky

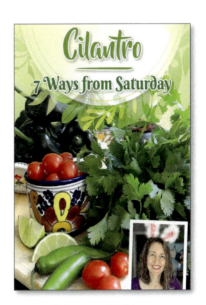

Cilantro, 7 Ways from Saturday

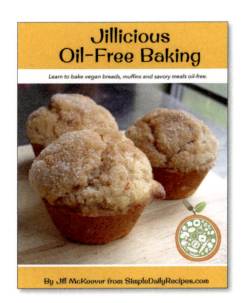

Jillicious Oil-Free Baking

OMGee Good! Soy Yogurt & Yogurt Recipes

Notes

Made in the USA
Middletown, DE
05 January 2024

47311522R00051